In The Dark ~~ ~~ of
Depression

A Journey through Anxiety, Depression & Post-Traumatic Stress Disorder

Julie Boyt

chipmunkapublishing
the mental health publisher

Julie Boyt

Published by
Chipmunkapublishing
United Kingdom

http://www.chipmunkapublishing.com

ISBN   978-1-78382-059-7

Chipmunkapublishing gratefully acknowledge the support of Arts Council England.

These poems are dedicated to the memory of
Jordan
A boy that I never knew
but will never forget

Julie Boyt

Preface

For the past few years, I have been unfortunate enough to suffer from a combination of anxiety, depression and post-traumatic stress disorder. I have found it very difficult to talk about my experiences to my family and friends during this time and I could never bring myself to recount my deepest thoughts or feelings to any of them.

I decided to describe my difficult journey through poetry and once I started writing, one poem just led onto another. Although I found it quite easy to write these poems, the thought that others will read them and discover my inner-most feelings, when I was in the dark depths of depression, is actually very scary! I am not ashamed of the depths of my illnesses; it's just that I have never wanted to admit how desperately ill I was to anyone else. I didn't want them to worry about me, so I always went out of my way to hide all evidence of how unwell I had actually become!

I hope that these poems can give a small insight into the thoughts and feelings that someone can have if they are affected by anxiety, depression or post-traumatic stress disorder. They are all conditions that can have hidden, invisible symptoms and are often not fully understood by those fortunate enough to have never been in their grips. Believe me though, if you become captured by any one of them, then it can feel that there will never be an escape from a very dark and disturbing world!

Julie Boyt

Before the darkness

It was a day in December, my favourite time of year
I was anticipating laughter and jolly festive cheer
The decorations were arranged, all matching and precise
The house smelled of cinnamon and aromatic Christmas spice
The tree was decorated, with lights that shined so bright
Twinkling and glistening, it was a beautiful magical sight

My shopping was complete; I'd bought the final toy
All preparations accomplished, this was a time of such joy
Mince pies were cooked and Christmas cards done
All that was left was to relax and have fun!
I had arranged a special party, full of festive pleasure
A night with friends that I would always treasure

My life back then, seems far in the distant past
Total contentment, which I presumed would always last
I wanted for nothing, had a family who were great
It was all so idyllic; as I was unaware of my fate
I would never have imagined, that this life would soon go on hold
I just wouldn't have believed it though, had I been foretold

Sadly this festive spirit, all joy to mankind
Was abruptly taken and celebrations left far behind
It all changed with an accident, that I so wished wasn't true
It was totally unexpected and just came out of the blue
This accident tragically took a young man's life away
And with it my happiness, changed to horror and dismay

~~~~~~~~~~

December had always been my favourite time of year and three
years ago, I was waiting with great excitement for all the Christmas
festivities to begin. My main concerns were deciding what food to
prepare, if I had bought enough coordinated decorations and other
similar frivolities. I was in such a fantastic mood and was so excited
to be going to a party that night with really special friends. My head
was full of joy and I was singing along to my favourite Christmas
carols as I drove off in my car to pick up my son from school.

The moment darkness fell

I was out in my car driving
On the never ending school run
Listening to the radio
Going to collect my youngest son

I suddenly saw a car on the verge
Dazed people were standing around
There was no screaming or shouting
Just eerie silence, without any sound

I asked if they wanted any help
They replied that they needed me quick
I approached the car, my nerves on edge
Hoping no-one was injured or sick

I looked through the driver's window
To a sight that was such a shock
A fence post had come through the windscreen
With the force of a giant rock

I just couldn't believe what I saw
A young lad in the driver's seat
He was unconscious and didn't look well
Staying calm was a difficult feat!

He still had a pulse; there was a glimmer of hope
But we needed to do something right now
We managed to pull him out through the window
To this day I will never know how

I quickly switched into medical mode
As a midwife, I was used to staying cool
However, my job was to welcome in new life
Not watch it go, in a way so cruel

I tried so hard to resuscitate him
With the help of an amazing man
I was pleading that he would take a breath
To let him go wasn't part of my plan

Seconds turned to minutes
But it seemed that time stood still
The three of us were fighting for life
We were fighting with all our will

Hope, sadly started to fade away
But I just couldn't accept defeat
We kept on going, kept on trying
Death, I was determined to cheat

I felt like I was with my own son
They both had a similar look
I stroked his face, said soothing words
And prayed that he wouldn't be took

I started to think of his family
And that dreaded knock on the door
When a policeman would give the tragic news
That they had lost the son they adore

When the emergency services began to arrive
We took a step back from the scene
That's when I crumbled, became a wreck
We'd failed to save the life of this teen

My legs were covered in scratches and stings
From the nettles and brambles that I had knelt
It was strange how I hadn't even noticed
Numbness was all that I had felt

I couldn't believe that he was gone
The whole experience didn't make sense
It couldn't be real, it couldn't be true
The reality was just too immense!

~~~~~~~~~~~~

This was the first time that I had been involved in a fatal accident and it was an event that I was totally unprepared for. Having worked in a hospital, in the medical profession, I was used to coping with regular emergencies. However, this accident was by far the most traumatic experience that I had ever encountered.

Even though I was initially in a state of total disbelief, I quickly switched into an automatic medical stance and my exterior appearance was one of total calm and professionalism. I had recently attended a first aid course and feel confident that if there had been any chance that the young man's life could have been saved, then we gave him that chance.

However, even though it appeared that I was physically coping, my feelings were totally frozen and it was as if I was strangely detached from the whole situation. I remember casually saying to the lovely man who was assisting me in the resuscitation "Oh dear, he's not going to make it - that's a bit of a shame!" I felt so emotionally numb as if it all wasn't actually real and I was just watching a scene on television. I think that this was the only way that my brain was able to cope with such a traumatic situation. It seemed to instantly shut down all of my emotions and awareness of any exterior stimuli so that I could totally focus my efforts on just physically trying to save him.

I now know that he was fatally injured on impact, so sadly any effort to save him wouldn't have enabled him to keep his life. However, even though I am aware of this knowledge, I have still felt that it was partially my fault that he died. Although irrational, I have been haunted by the fear that I didn't do a good enough job and that if I had tried harder he may have survived.

I do take condolence though, that we were with him at the end and that I was able to give him some tender words and a loving touch as he passed on. If it had been my son, then I would have wanted someone to have tried to help him and for him not to have been all alone during his last living moments on this earth.

Life should continue

Life should continue
Life should evolve
Life should be something to behold
Life should develop
Life should persist
Life should remain until you are old

Accidents shouldn't happen
Accidents shouldn't occur
Accidents shouldn't affect the young
Accidents shouldn't arise
Accidents shouldn't befall
Accidents shouldn't take life just begun

Death doesn't discriminate
Death doesn't choose
Death doesn't pick who it takes
Death doesn't worry
Death doesn't care
Death doesn't forgive major mistakes

Despair will follow
Despair will ensue
Despair will take over your mind
Despair will engulf
Despair will destroy
Despair will make peace hard to find

~~~~~~~~~~

Sadly fatal accidents can happen to anyone and at any time. It is natural to hope that we will never be involved in such a traumatic event, or that it will affect anyone that we are close to. It would be very destructive to constantly fear such a frightening event, so although I knew that it could theoretically happen; I had always hoped and presumed that it wouldn't.

Although I was amazingly calm during the actual accident, I quickly went into total shock. It was unbelievable that I had just watched a boy lose his life and my brain really couldn't accept that this was true. I tried to stay strong and not let the trauma impact on my everyday life, but this proved to be totally impossible. I ended up spiralling downhill very rapidly, as it felt that my heart and soul had been smashed into a thousand pieces. Even though I was feeling so terrible, I still wouldn't accept that I wasn't able to cope, and tried to pretend to myself and everyone else that I was actually doing really well!

Denial and pretence

I am fine
I am good
I am feeling rather well
I am better
I am recovered
The truth, I'd rather not dwell

I can laugh
I can giggle
I can behave exactly the same
I can smile
I can chuckle
Pretence is my favourite game

I still talk
I still gossip
I still tell the odd joke
I still chat
I still natter
Empty words that are often spoke

I'm not stressed
I'm not anxious
I'm not suffering on my own
I'm not troubled
I'm not worried
My true feelings are never shown

I feel calmness
I feel serenity
I feel stillness in my mind
I feel relaxed
I feel tranquillity
But peace is impossible to find

I want recovery
I want harmony
I want an ending to this pain
I want healing
I want closure
To enjoy my life once again

~~~~~~~~~~

Looking back, I still find it hard to comprehend that I was simply not aware of how ill I had become. I honestly thought that I was fine and didn't have any problems! My head still simply wouldn't acknowledge my illnesses, although those people who were close to me were beginning to see through my elaborate acts!

As time went by and I became more unwell, I found it increasingly difficult to disguise my true thoughts and feelings. This continual pretence left me totally exhausted and I found it all so mentally draining. I started to dread meeting up with anyone, as it was so much easier to just stay at home by myself, where I felt safe to be miserable and sad!

Sliding into depression

It all started with an accident
A boy who lost his life
I tried so hard to save him
But in vain was all my strife

I couldn't cope with the memories
The pictures that came at night
I tried to block out the upsetting scenes
All the images of his sad plight

I thought it best to bury my thoughts
To erase them from my mind
I hoped that the trauma would go away
But it did nothing of the kind

My life changed so dramatically
I was experiencing constant stress
Everything just bothered me
My head was in total distress

I tried to carry on as before
Only my smiles were now an act
I pretended that I was coping well
But sincerity, my behaviour just lacked

As weeks passed by and turned to months
The pain became too much to bear
I spiralled downhill, felt out of control
Positive thoughts became so rare

I became a recluse in my bedroom
Listening to the same song every day
I blanked out the world around me
On my own, I just wanted to stay

I wouldn't talk to my family
Couldn't bear to feel their touch
I just wanted them to leave me alone
Even a cuddle was all too much

Daily jobs became neglected
My husband took over them all
I couldn't be bothered to do anything
Under my duvet, I wanted to crawl

I was in denial that I was mentally ill
With conditions that all had a name
I thought that I just wasn't coping
That my inadequacies were all to blame

I was embarrassed to have become unwell
It was something my mind tried to hide
I pretended that I was feeling fine
And in myself, I refused to confide

My doctor prescribed some 'happy pills'
She saw that I was clearly in need
I wasn't overly keen on taking them
But her advice, I decided to heed

I was sure that I would never recover
I could see no light amongst the dark
My life was full of despair and gloom
As the trauma had left such a mark

It felt that two lives had ended
On that fateful day last year
My previous self, so calm and fun
Now engulfed in anxiety and fear

~~~~~~~~~~

Mental illness was something that I had never really given much thought to, prior to the accident and it was a subject that I was really quite ignorant about. I had always felt empathy and compassion towards anyone who was suffering from it though.
I knew that it was something that unfortunately can still carry such a stigma in our society and many people feel that they have to hide their illness and problems away.
Because it something that cannot be seen and is often not on public display, it is a topic that can be very easy to ignore. People generally don't talk about their depression or other mental health conditions in their everyday conversations and I was as guilty as the next person in not really wanting to talk or think about such topics! Therefore, because of my lack of awareness, it was totally unexpected when I started to deteriorate and go downhill so quickly. It felt pretty scary to have virtually no control over my mind, or the negative thoughts that I constantly dwelled upon. I was entering all sorts of dark and disturbing places that my head had

never visited before and were places that I really would have preferred not to have gone to at all!

This new world all felt very alien to me. Having always been such a happy and positive person, I never dreamed that I would ever suffer from any type of mental illness myself. I was so wrong though, to think that I would never be "That type of person!"

The turmoil in my head

My head is hurting, it is pounding all day
This persistent turmoil, never subsiding away
I am constantly struggling, always in pain
It continues to wreck havoc, inside of my brain
Its powerful grip, seems to clamp down so tight
Giving me no respite, during the day or at night
It is so disturbing and can awaken me from any dream
Because its effects are so frightening, distressing and extreme
I have tried taking painkillers, with sadly no effect
As they can't calm a head, that's messed up and wrecked!

This pain is not a typical headache that you generally find
Nor is it a migraine, that's troubling my mind
There is no point having a consultation with my GP
As all her examinations, would just confirm and agree
That nothing would show on x-ray, or on any other scan
As it was witnessing the accident, when this trauma all began
There are no physical problems, lurking deep down inside
It is all due to the memories, which I desperately try to hide
This turmoil will continue though, today and tomorrow
As the cause of my anguish, stems from tragedy and sorrow

I am sure that all this turmoil, is starting to grow and swell
Is trying to break out, from its internal captive cell
If only I could tame this turbulence, inside of my head
As this persistent rage, is something that I now fear and dread
If only I could achieve respite and a moment of release
I would then find calmness and my agonies might all cease
The solution is to unlock these images, which I have deleted out
As this is the true cause of my problems, I know without a doubt
For the memories to magically disappear is all that I ever hope
Because if I had to retrieve them, I know that I wouldn't cope!

~~~~~~~~~~

Throughout this time, it felt that my body was living in a constant
state of stress and anxiety, with high levels of adrenaline
continuously surging around my body. I am not sure whether it was
the effects of all of these stress hormones that caused the feelings
of pressure inside of my head, or if it was just the raw pain of grief
and despair. Whatever the cause though, it was relentless and
made everything so much harder to cope with!

Julie Boyt

Living with post-traumatic stress disorder

I have post-traumatic stress disorder
The title my condition is assigned
Disorder is such a suitable name
As it is exactly the state of my mind

I thought this condition only affected soldiers
Returning from the horrors of war
I never dreamed that it could be so devastating
Or would destroy the life that I adore

At first I denied that I had anything wrong
Carried on in my usual way
I tried to bury my disturbing thoughts
Shutting away that fateful day

My main symptom was avoidance
I would refuse to think of that poor lad
I buried the trauma deep down in my brain
Locked away things distressing and sad

I avoided contact with my family
Refused them entry into my plight
I would hardly utter a single word
Stayed hidden and out of sight

I felt I was always running on stress
My adrenaline levels were so high
I saw danger in every direction I looked
Convinced someone else would soon die

This constant stress caused continuous tears
I would sob even though nothing was sad
I always feared things would turn out the worst
That those outcomes would always be bad

My brain went into shutdown
It couldn't cope with the outside world
My mind just retreated in on itself
Only, my thoughts still constantly whirled

Sleep was so troubled, that I dreaded the night
As that was when my brain would dig deep
Bringing up all those memories suppressed
Into my dreams, the nightmares would creep

I would then get up to exercise
Something I had previously thought of with dread
I loved to walk in the middle of the night
In the moonlight, I would frequently tread

I was unable to relax, or ever let go
I found it impossible to totally unwind
Always fearing those dreaded flashbacks
The ones that tormented my mind

For some lucky few, things improve after a while
But for others it can continue for years
As its name implies, its effects are traumatic
It has caused me such anguish and tears

~~~~~~~~~~~

I had previously heard of post-traumatic stress disorder and knew that it was a condition that affected people who had been involved in, or witnessed, a traumatic event. I had never known anyone who had suffered from it before though, so I was unaware of the many symptoms and effects that it can have.

When I initially started to feel unwell, I searched on the internet for more information and could identify with most of the symptoms relating to post-traumatic stress disorder. Even though my symptoms exactly matched those that were described, I still didn't believe that I was suffering from it at all! I couldn't accept that I had anything wrong with me and in hind sight; I think that I just wasn't ready to admit to myself that I was mentally unwell. I was a strong person who had always coped with everything that came my way, so of course this wasn't going to be something that I would be affected by!

Elusive sleep

Exhausted and shattered
I am desperate for sleep
I would do anything for some rest
I try shutting my eyes
Tell my body to relax
But cannot drift off into release

Sheep are passing me by
I count them as they jump
But still my mind wanders on
I try creating a tranquil void
But this emptiness never appears
As my thoughts just won't be ignored

I've had a mug of cocoa to drink
And a warm soothing bath
Soft music is all around
I follow gentle routines
The books say this helps
So soon, I should be snoozing away

But, I am still lying here awake
It's the middle of the night
Where is this elusive sleep?
I'm going to have to give up all hope
And reluctantly rise from my bed
And accept, that I am beaten again

I am so tired during the day though
And then desperate for sleep
I could snooze at the drop of a hat
But when darkness returns
My brain seems to spring back to life
All ready for its evening fight!

Hooray, at long last
My eyes wearily droop
And into the land of nod I tread
Soon in my dreams though
A terrifying nightmare appears
And destroys my last hope of sleep!

~~~~~~~~

I had always taken sleep for granted and had never previously had any problems falling asleep, only getting up again in the mornings! I found it quite alien to be lying awake for hours, exhausted, but unable to relax and calm my thoughts. It was very frustrating to be in bed in a wide awake state, whilst my husband was lying next to me, blissfully snoozing the night away!

I feel stressed, I feel anxious

I feel stressed
So stressed
It's messing with my brain
I have stress
Such stress
I will never smile again

I feel anxious
So anxious
It's out of control
I have anxiety
Such anxiety
It's really taking its toll

I feel troubled
So troubled
Deep down in my heart
I have troubles
Such troubles
It's tearing me apart

I feel nauseous
So nauseous
I think I will be sick
I have nausea
Such nausea
Bring a bowl to me quick!

I feel panicky
So panicky
Negativity is my only thought
I have panics
Such panics
I always feel distraught

I feel worried
So worried
I am running out of hope
I have worries
Such worries
I really cannot cope!

~~~~~~~~~~

This is a poem that I wrote one day when I was feeling really stressed and anxious and it was a feeling that became so familiar to me whilst I was unwell! I had always been a very relaxed and easy going person and had never suffered from high levels of stress or anxiety before. It therefore came as quite a surprise, when my body started to show signs of severe anxiety in ordinary everyday situations, such as going to the shops or walking my dogs. I started to notice many disturbing physical symptoms such as a racing heartbeat, dizziness, awful nausea and a tight constriction around my throat.

I could never predict when I would experience one of these anxiety attacks and they didn't seem to follow any patterns, so I was always on my guard waiting for the next one to occur!

I also started to continuously worry about everyone and everything. My thoughts were always concentrating on the negative aspects of things, rather than the positive and I was sure that everything would always end up with the worst possible outcome!

Understandably, all this anxiety and worry made it virtually impossible to ever rest and relax, as my mind just wouldn't be stilled and I felt so exhausted from it all. Eventually I started to feel so tired and lethargic throughout the day, that I was unable to participate in general everyday life any more.

Julie Boyt

I am not depressed

I am not depressed
What do you mean?
Your words are making me sad
You may watch me crying
And sobbing most of the time
But I am normally happy and glad!

I am not depressed
I don't accept your view
I am tired only some of the time
I suffer from insomnia
So need to stay in my bed
But the occasional nap is hardly a crime!

I am not depressed
Is that what you think?
I know that I am coping just fine
I may have been drinking
It helps numb the pain
But it's only the odd tipple of wine!

I am not depressed
Don't talk that way
I just have a few chores to address
I know I haven't tidied up yet
Or cleaned anything for a while
But the house looks lived in, not just a mess!

I am not depressed
You make things up
I am continuing my daily routine
No, I haven't done my hair yet
Or had time to brush my teeth
But I really keep tidy and clean!

I am not depressed
How can you say that?
I am caring for myself, can't you tell?
Ok, I may not have showered
Or had a bath for a week
But my perfume disguises my smell!

I am not depressed
Please get real
I sing in the morning as I dress
Well, I may still be in pyjamas
Yes, I've had these on all week
But they're the comfiest clothes I possess!

I am not depressed
I am chilled and relaxed
In a constant state of calm
Sometimes I scream and shout
And smash things against the wall
But I honestly don't mean any harm!

I am not depressed
You are annoying me now
Believe me when I say I'm not down
I may not go out with you
For a walk or to the shops
But I often drive myself into town!

I am not depressed
Just leave me alone
I want you to go away
I am fed up of explaining
Telling you that I am well
I really don't want you to stay!

I am not depressed
Don't phone or text
Your questioning makes me feel bad
I know that you care for me
You persist because you are concerned
But what you're doing is driving me mad!

~~~~~~~~~~

When I was at my worst, those close to me were obviously concerned about my behaviour as they could see that I was acting very out of character. If they ever voiced their concerns though, I would instantly deny everything and would make up all sorts of excuses to justify my unusual behaviour. Why did they keep suggesting that I was depressed and needed help? Of course I wasn't depressed! Their persistent questioning and suggestions made me very agitated and I became so annoyed by it all. I used to think "No wonder I am spending all of my time in bed", as it was the only place that I could escape from everyone's concerns and be totally left alone!

You look so great

It is actually quite ironic
Everyone used to say
You're looking really great
You've got so thin
Amazingly trim
You've lost a lot of weight

The truth be told
I hated food
My diet had spiralled downhill
But because I was slim
They said I looked well
When in fact, I was chronically ill

It all seemed very bizarre
That I used to get stopped
To be told that I looked so cool
You appear really happy
You are amazingly calm
So this persona became my new rule

It seemed really strange
To get these comments
When all I felt was stress
They thought that I was coping
Taking it all in my stride
When I was actually in total distress

I really couldn't believe it
My friends would sometimes say
You look the best we've ever known
Although inside I was crumbling
My mind in a mess
But these true feelings would never be shown

Appearances can be deceptive
Often not what they seem
Real feelings pushed away to hide
If they had looked behind the mask
They would have seen through my disguise
To a person who was screaming inside!

~~~~~~~~~~

My slimmer figure was constantly associated with well-being during this time and I was often told that I looked so great and well. It felt very ironic, that previously when I was actually feeling brilliant but a couple of dress sizes bigger; I had rarely received any such compliments! I would always smile and say thanks for their kind words and agree that I was indeed feeling really good!

It felt very strange though, that loosing this much weight so quickly was seen as a sign of achievement, rather than a sign of how ill I had actually become. It was one of the few outward signs of the seriousness of my depressive state. However, it was one that was misinterpreted by the majority of the people that I met as a sign of good health and wellness, when in fact I was feeling the worst that I had ever felt in my entire life!

I can't carry on

I want a way out
I can't carry on
I've really had enough
I'm sick of this darkness
I'm fed up of life
I'm really not calling your bluff

What have I got left here?
Why should I stay?
There's nothing for me to do
My head's full of worries
My hearts full of pain
I hope that you believe this is true

But how shall I do it?
What shall I choose?
A way that will cause least distress
I could write a long note
Or leave you a message
So my reasons, you won't have to guess

I just need some courage
I should do it right now
There is no reason left to wait
But will you forgive me?
Will you understand?
My memory, I don't want you to hate

My boys are my treasures
My husband too
I would leave them all behind
I am feeling quite guilty
They would all suffer and mourn
Am I being selfish and just unkind?

Maybe there are different options?
Other things to try
Solutions I do not yet know
I am losing my courage
Is it really my time?
Perhaps I am not ready to go?

~~~~~~~~~~

Living in such total despair, that a person feels that there is only one way out, is a very sad and uncomfortable thought. It is one of the ultimate taboos in many societies, including our own and is a silent subject that is usually ignored. Nobody speaks of it and nobody would voice their desire to do it, unless they were exceptionally brave!

In the mental health profession, there is an in-depth understanding of this subject and if such thoughts were mentioned then there would be a reaction of empathy, rather than one of horror! They know that these thoughts are really common amongst the depressed and they understand that it is a topic that can continuously whirl around in your head, even if you don't want it to.

Fortunately, I never got to the stage where I was close to taking my own life, but that didn't stop my imagination from running away with itself! The intensity and frequency of these thoughts increased as I became more unwell and they were actually pretty scary and frightening in themselves!

This dark contemplation made me feel so guilty though and I am sure that this guilt made my depressive state worse in itself. This then led to an increase in my negative thoughts and subsequent guilt, so it actually all turned into a perpetuating vicious circle!

Before I became unwell, I had always presumed that such thoughts were very rare and I was so surprised to find out how common they actually are. Thankfully, for the majority of people, including myself, they remain only thoughts and do not turn into desperate actions.

I now have a far greater understanding of how someone could so easily get to that stage, where they genuinely feel that there is no other way out. Living under a persistent, intolerable black cloud can be enough to push even the most sensible person to take extreme measures to escape!

Pull yourself together girl

Pull yourself together girl
Why are you behaving this way?
You've had ages now to recover
It's been far too long, is all I can say

These are the types of comments I received
By a person, I thought of as a friend
She would drop remarks into conversations
Did she hope that I could magically mend?

I can't believe you're not over it yet
Why are you acting so weird?
You need to find your inner strength
Then life won't be as bad as you've feared

Please think about what you are saying
They may only be small words that you blurt
But each comment you say, increases my pain
Every sentence just adds to my hurt

Pull yourself together girl
You've had plenty of time to get well
I don't know why you are still crying?
You have no reason to constantly dwell

I cry because I am so unhappy
They are not just crocodile tears
I have lost the ability to turn off my tap
And your opinions just add to my fears

I am surprised that you are still like this
You can't think that you are still ill?
Just hurry up and get better
Get onto that road downhill

It hurts to be told such unkind things
Doesn't she know she is making me worse?
If only I could wish my worries away
I would wish them all to disperse

Pull yourself together girl
You're just lazing around like a slob
You're joking; you're not still signed off sick?
You should definitely be back at your job

I hate it that I am not able to work
I miss all of my colleagues and friends
Being a midwife is a role that I so adore
And I will be devastated if it ever ends

I hope you aren't pulling a fast one
I think you've got a bit of a cheek
It's about time that you toughened up
As you are behaving so pathetic and weak

Just because you cannot see that I am ill
Doesn't mean that I have recovered inside
Why do you judge, when you haven't a clue?
Why voice these thoughts that I can't abide?

~~~~~~~~~~

The majority of comments that I received from my friends and colleagues were ones that were very encouraging and supportive. However, there were a few people that I knew that would drop the odd hurtful comment into conversations, or would say negative remarks behind my back.

Of course, they weren't aware of how ill I had become, or the daily struggles that I faced. To them it seemed obvious that all I needed to do was to "Pull myself together" and I would magically recover!

Shortly after I had been signed off sick, a colleague told my friend that she would "Never go off sick with something as trivial as stress!" and that "There is no place in our profession for people who are affected by stress!" Exactly what I needed to hear at a time when I was feeling so vulnerable and low!

All of these negative comments would really upset me and would make me so sad, that I often sobbed uncontrollably after hearing them. It all made me feel so ashamed to be unwell with a mental illness and just reinforced the belief that it was all due to my weakness and lack of strength that I had not recovered sooner!

Please Mum

Please come here mum
Just to play
Where have you got to?
It's like you've run away

Please go into the garden mum
Just walk outside
Step out of your bedroom
Do you have to always hide?

Please talk to us mum
Just a natter
Listen to our worries
React to our chatter

Please read to us mum
Just one book
You used to tell us stories
At pictures we would look

Please make us dinner mum
Just any food
If we ask you to make some
You are never in the mood

Pleased don't get stressed mum
Just calm down
You appear really anxious
You always wear a frown

Please don't cry mum
Just the odd tear
We know you're constantly sobbing
It's a sound we often hear

Please give us a cuddle mum
Just one touch
We used to love your snuggles
We miss them ever so much

Please show us affection mum
Just some tender care
Do you even still like us?
Have you any love left to share?

Please get better mum
Just be well
You used to be such fun
Now you only mope and dwell

Please come back to us mum
Just be our rock
We'd do anything for our old mum
Oh please rewind the clock

~~~~~~~~~~~

I felt great guilt and always will, that my family suffered so much throughout my illness. When I was at my worst, it felt that I was living inside a really small bubble that had virtually no access to anyone else. I would very occasionally let my family and friends come inside, but this was really infrequent and would be for a limited time only. I was aware that I was pushing everyone out of my life though and it made me feel terrible. However, I was incapable of behaving in any other way, as I could only cope by staying totally isolated and by being left alone.

Watching and living alongside someone who is mentally unwell can be extremely hard and traumatic in itself. I know that my family found it very difficult, especially as my illnesses continued for three years, rather than only a couple of weeks or months.

There was always uncertainty surrounding everything that we did throughout this time as well. Nothing could be planned in case I felt too unwell to leave the house, or even to leave my bed! My family also had to live with the uncertainty of when, or indeed if, I would ever recover again!

My best friend

My best friend, you are truly wonderful
The bestest friend that I have ever known
I wouldn't have got through these dark times
Without all the love that you have shown

In those dark times you were my lifeline
You were the rope that held me back
Whenever I felt that I was falling down
Into a hole so deep and black

Nothing was ever too much for you
By my side you would always stand
Whenever I felt that I needed you
You would be there to hold my hand

You had this ability to understand
As if telepathic when you were near
You always understood my unspoken words
And though this silence, you could always hear

I knew you saw through my disguise
So I had no need to pretend or be brave
I didn't have to hide my illness away
As support is all that you gave

I was so grateful that you still visited
When I was just miserable to be near
I emitted an aura of negativity
Was lacking in fun and cheer

But you never minded how I behaved
Even when I became quite adverse
You never judged, you only accepted
You were a friend, for better or worse

A shoulder to cry on, the saying goes
Well I've drenched your shoulders with tears
When sobbing you would calm me down
Reduced or vanquished my fears

Your life is so busy and hectic though
With no hours left to spare
But you always find that extra time
To show me such love and care

My best friend, I wouldn't be without you
You are helping me to reach my goal
I will always love you forever
You are part of my heart and soul

~~~~~~~~~~~

I am so very lucky to have many amazing best friends, who have all been so wonderful to me throughout this time and I would be totally lost without them all.

Debbie is one of my best friends, and I definitely wouldn't have been able to cope with the last three years without her. She has always been there for me, at any time, no matter what. She would regularly phone, text and visit to see how I was and I felt that she really cared about me. With her, I didn't have to reply to the standard question "How are you?" with "I'm fine". She wouldn't have believed that answer anyway!

There was hardly anyone that I felt comfortable enough to be my true self and to say what I was really thinking. With her though, I could voice all of my worries and concerns and know that I would get only empathy, understanding and support in return!

As her name suggests; she is just simply the BEST.

The darkness of depression

Darkness, darkness all around
All I see is black
I've fallen into a deep dark hole
And cannot find my way back

Darkness, darkness everywhere
I wish I could see some light
I try so hard to leave this gloom
I try with all my might

Darkness, darkness surrounding me
I feel I am so alone
It's like I'm totally by myself
I'm crying on my own

Darkness, darkness smothering me
I'm struggling with this pain
I'm not sure I can carry on
I feel that I'm going insane

Darkness, darkness trapping me
No-one hears me shout
I think I'm stuck in here forever
There is no path to get out

Darkness, darkness in the sky
I'm staring at the night
Gradually, I can see some stars
What a wonderful, welcome sight

Darkness, darkness, but not so dark
I'm sure I can see the dawn
The sun is rising, a chink of light
I can smile, and not just mourn

Darkness, darkness fading away
Brightness is replacing the black
My life of joy had disappeared
Now I'm finally enticing it back

~~~~~~~~~~

This is a poem that I wrote a couple of years ago, for my friend
Claire. She was finding life really hard and I felt sure that she was

on the verge of entering a very gloomy dark place. I wanted to give her inspiration and show her that however difficult things seemed at the time, there was always hope and light waiting for her just around the corner.

italk – Guiding me out of the darkness into the light

I felt that I had been in the darkness forever
I was sure that I would never leave it behind
I had been searching for an invisible exit
Given up hope of a doorway to find

I am sure that I would never have recovered
Had I not been lucky enough to read
About a therapy service called italk
Which looked perfect for my current need

It was a self-referral service
For those who were depressed
Or anyone who needed additional support
If they were anxious, low or stressed

I phoned the number stated
Discussed the history of my past year
CBT was to be the therapy of choice
At a location that was local and near

My first visit was organised
I was really nervous and just not sure
But I so wanted to become well again
That I would have done anything for a cure

I was to meet with one of their therapists
A high intensity one they said
I really didn't mind what her title was
If only she could sort out my troubled head

The day approached when we were to meet
I wished I had not signed up at all
I was so anxious, that I just felt sick
Debated cancelling with a simple call

I needn't have had these concerns though
As she instantly put me at ease
Her manner was so calm and caring
And my worries she tried to appease

She explained my many symptoms
Gave me insight into why I behaved this way
She also sat quietly and listened
To all the things that I wanted to say

Each session I was set different homework
Its difficulty was steadily increased
My hardest task was reliving the accident
Until its impact just gradually ceased

I went back to see her every week
It became the highlight of my day
She had this ability to lift my low spirits
Gave inspiration with all that she would say

My time in therapy was like a roller coaster
One week I would be up, the next week down
My therapist never knew what to expect
Whether a smile or a miserable frown

I was so pleased that I had plucked up the courage
Been brave enough to seek advice
I finally had optimism that my life would change
Not to amazing or fantastic, but just nice

As time went by, I started to improve
Just taking tiny steps at the start
Over time my fears began to reduce
And less adrenaline surged to my heart

I was given ways of coping
Because of course, I still suffered from stress
But when this occurred, I could calm right down
Be in control, not in my usual distress

My nightmares became less violent
Occasionally replaced with a happy dream
It was amazing to finally wake up
Without a cold sweat or a terrified scream

As my sessions began to draw to a close
I felt sad that they were coming to their end
It had been a special time, when I could be myself
Where I had no desire or need to pretend

I have now completed all of my sessions
They have healed the despair in my mind
They have enabled me to move out of the dark
And leave my trauma and anguish behind

~~~~~~~~~~

I was so anxious about starting these italk sessions, that I almost changed my mind about turning up altogether. I had spent so long pretending that I was well to other people, that I was scared at the thought of sharing my true thoughts and feelings with a stranger.

I had also previously had a different form of therapy with a private therapist, but had seen no real improvement in my condition. Because of this, I really didn't have high expectations of these italk sessions at all and was doubtful that they would actually be able to help me to recover.

On the morning of my appointment, I felt so stressed and apprehensive that I nearly phoned up to cancel all of my therapy sessions, so that I wouldn't have to attend. Fortunately, something inside of my head stopped me from doing this and I managed to persuade myself that I should pluck up the courage to at least give them one try. I am so pleased that I listened to my intuition, as since attending these CBT sessions, my life has changed beyond all recognition. I have now recovered immeasurably and am getting so much closer to becoming the happy and confident person that I used to be before the accident. I am just so glad that I decided to be brave and attend this therapy, as it was probably one of the best decisions that I have ever made!

I will always be an advocate of italk, and cannot speak highly enough of its brilliant services. If I hadn't been fortunate enough to have come across a leaflet advertising italk, and referred myself, then I am sure that my story would have had a totally different ending!

On the other side of depression

I really can't believe it
I am finally on the mend
My dreams have now been answered
As my illnesses are at their end

I am now so very happy
My anguish has vanished away
I no longer live in continuous stress
Or have emotions that are all astray

I am able to get up in the mornings
Instead of hibernating in bed
I can look forward to each new day
And not fear the dawn with such dread

I am also able to enjoy small pleasures
Like the singing of the birds
They seem to be busy chattering away
Without actually saying any words

I no longer worry about doing nothing
Or just sitting wasting time
If it's relaxing and therapeutic
It can hardly be seen as a crime

I really love meeting up with all my friends
No longer feeling the need to pretend
I can now voice what's on my mind
As my pretence has come to its end

I have also removed my trusty disguise
Flung off my faithful mask
I am open and honest to all I know
To accept me is all that I now ask

It feels so wonderful to interact again
Not to be isolated on my own
I have rejoined my family life once more
No longer solitary and all alone

The boys love having their mother back
Not the grumpy person who was in her place
They now have lots of my affection
Many a hug and tender embrace

In The Dark Depths of Depression

These cuddles are so soothing
They calm me right down to the core
Endorphins surge around my body
A feeling I love and adore

My adrenaline levels have subsided
I am not so anxious and wound up tight
I no longer have that knot in my stomach
Or feel sick from morning until night

Because of this though, my appetite has returned
My wonderful diet has all but gone
It would be great if I could stay so slim
But the weight is bound to go back on

But it doesn't really matter
If I increase in size and weight
I will no longer get any compliments
Or be told that I really look great

Because now I can't stop smiling
I feel fabulous and oh so well
What counts is how you feel inside
As your body is only your shell

It feels so good to have returned to the light
No longer existing in the dark
This experience has been so traumatic though
That I will always be carrying its mark

I am not pretending that it is all easy
That I never feel sad and low
But when this occurs, I just give myself time
And then take things steady and slow

I know that I will always suffer from stress
But I will not let it get me down
Because mostly I am calm and relaxed
Now a happy person to be around

I am so grateful to have finally recovered
Thank you for allowing me to mend
I will always be so appreciative
That my dark days have come to their end

~~~~~~~~~~

I am so lucky to have got my life back again, as at one stage I was sure that I would always be living in the dark shadows of anxiety, depression and post-traumatic stress disorder.

I really didn't appreciate just how good my life was before I became unwell and it was only when it was taken away from me that I realised how fantastic it all was. Although my life will never be the same again, I am fortunate to now have the opportunity to lead a fun and enjoyable life, instead of barely existing from one day to the next. I have more time to stop and enjoy the small everyday pleasures that I used to take for granted and I really appreciate how good it is just to be alive on this earth!

I would now like to spend my time as a mental health advocate, helping and supporting others who are unlucky enough to also be in the grips of mental ill health. I hope that my experience and insight can allow me to offer empathy and understanding to others in a similar situation. I am so excited about this new life and all the various possibilities that a future in the mental health profession can bring and I really can't wait for it all to begin!

It feels wonderful to be able to now look forward, as during my darkest days I really didn't think that I would have a future at all. I could see no further than just trying to make it through that particular, difficult day. To have this chance of a new and fulfilling life is actually quite unexpected, but just so wonderful and I intend to fully embrace it with open arms!

When I was in the dark depths of depression, I was convinced that I was such a weak and pathetic person for allowing my mind and life to be taken over. I now think the opposite though and anyone who has struggled, or is currently struggling, should be very proud of themselves. It takes such courage and bravery to have to face the darkness, as it can be a very scary and disturbing place!

To those who are currently in the dark depths of depression

If you currently have depression
Feel anxious, stressed or low
Then this book is especially for you
I would love it to give inspiration
That you also can become well
I hope that you believe this is true

It would be great if these poems
Offer a small glimmer of hope
That your happiness can grow yet again
That there can be an escape
From your life full of despair
That you won't always be suffering this pain

But you have to hang on in there
Try to hold on tight
And don't let your life be consumed
You can get through this
You have the ability to succeed
Then your life can again be resumed

If you find that you are struggling
Try to seek some support
A person with whom you can confide
It can really make a difference
If you can share things with a friend
And know you have a comrade by your side

If you take antidepressants
Do not feel bad
There is definitely no need to feel shame
They are part of your armour
A weapon to be used
To help conquer this battle and game

Don't be hard on yourself
Don't beat yourself up
This is not something that you personally chose
Nobody would wish for this
It's awful feeling so bad
I just hope your darkness soon goes

Try to take things gently though
Aim for small little steps
As recovery can be frustratingly slow
But the seeds of peace and happiness
Are deep inside your mind
Just waiting to flourish and grow

~~~~~~~~~~

With eternal thanks

To all of the fantastic people who have helped me to get through this dark time. I am so lucky to have had the support of all of my great friends and family, as without them, my struggles would have been so much harder to cope with.
Extra special thanks though, must be given to these extra special people:

Graham – My wonderful husband, who I totally adore

Stuart, Jamie and Alex – My absolute treasures

Amanda, Angela, Annette, Beverley, Dawn, Debbie, Gabbie, Helen, Lauren, Rachael, Maggie, and Sam - I love all of you so much

Dr Lambert – The kindest doctor that I have ever known

Helen and Vanessa – Two amazing therapists, who have guided me out of the depths of despair and darkness

Sarah and Vanessa – For supporting me, as I take my first steps towards a future career in mental health

The Recovery College – For their brilliant courses and facilitators who are all "Holding the Hope!"

italk - A fantastic service that I was so fortunate to find out about. Without it, I am sure that I would never have recovered and would probably still be stuck in bed right now!

Julie Boyt

with very best wishes

julie x

Lightning Source UK Ltd.
Milton Keynes UK
UKOW03f2010180314

228375UK00001B/3/P